BUGS

Ants, Beetles, Caterpillars, & More!

Carus Publishing Company
Peterborough, NH
www.cricketmag.com

Staff
Editorial Director: Lou Waryncia
Project Editor: Charles Baker III
Designer: Brenda Ellis, Graphic Sense
Proofreader: Eileen Terrill

Text Credits
The content of this volume is derived from articles that first appeared in *CLICK*®, *APPLESEEDS*, and *ODYSSEY*™ magazines. Contributors: Stephen Buchmann ("Working the Night Shift"), Mary Salmon Kennedy ("Don't Wash That Dirt Away"), Gretchen Noyes-Hull ("An Eye for Ants"), Charnan Simon ("Laurel's Rainforest").

Picture Credits
Photos.com: 4, 28; Paige Billin-Frye: 5; Visuals Unlimited: 6; Carol Hughes/Bruce Coleman: 7; Kirsten Guerin: 8–9; Paul Mirocha: 10–15; Pamela Carroll: 16–17; David Shaw: 18–19, 21; Marcy Ramsey: 22–27.

Cover
Dynamic Graphics

The Library of Congress Cataloging-in-Publication Data for *Bugs* is available at http://catalog.loc.gov.

Carus Publishing
30 Grove Street, Peterborough, NH 03458
www.cricketmag.com

Printed in China

Table of Contents

Yum!

Scaly Wing

They are called *Lepidoptera* (lep-i-DOP-ter-ah), or "scaly wing" by scientists. People call them daggerwings and checkerspots, buckeyes and brushfoots. There are more than 15,000 kinds of these creatures, and they live in almost every corner of the world. They have furry bodies and hairy pads on their six feet. They trick their enemies with camouflage. When that trick fails, some use poison. Their four wings come in every color of the rainbow and more. Their hollow tongues rest in a spiral, waiting to uncoil and sip their next meal. But they don't use these fancy tongues for tasting. They taste with their foot hairs!

Some live for just a few days. Others as long as 18 months. Many never leave their birthplace. Some may fly 2,000 miles. In the Amazon region, there are thousands of different kinds. They change from egg to caterpillar to chrysalis to their final life. What are these fantastic creatures? They're BUTTERFLIES, some of the most amazing insects on earth!

Day and Night in the Desert

In late spring, the desert is very hot and dry. But it is full of life. During the cool night, a beautiful saguaro cactus flower blossoms. In the morning, painted lady butterflies suck nectar from wildflowers growing in the sun.

5

Animal Eyes

Flying insects need good eyesight to see where they're going. This horsefly's eyes cover almost its entire head. If you look closely, you can see that its two giant eyes are made up of thousands of tiny eyes. All those eyes give horseflies a pretty good look at the world.

6

It's a Ball!

Are these beetles playing ball? Not exactly. They're dung beetles, and they are preparing their favorite food.

All over the world, dung beetles do a really important clean-up job. They eat the droppings of plant-eating animals, such as cows, sheep, zebras, and even elephants.

Eating dung may sound strange, but dung is mostly undigested food. It's filled with nutritious seeds and pieces of plants and fruit. Dung beetles use the sharp, tooth-like edges on their legs and heads to cut off a piece they like. They have to work fast — there are lots of beetles that want some dung. To keep a piece for themselves, they often shape it into a ball and roll the ball away to bury it in a safe place to eat later.

At mating time, a female beetle may ride on top of the ball as the male pushes. After they've buried the ball and mated underground, the female lays a single egg on top. That way her baby will have plenty of good dung to eat when it hatches.

Yum!

Just a little to the left, no right, no left again!

Don't Wash That Dirt Away

"Aw, Mom," a boy groans. He doesn't want a bath. His sister is not happy when told to wash her dirty hands. Would everyone be happy if there were no dirt? Not farmers. They couldn't plant their corn. Not earthworms. They couldn't dig their holes.

An earthworm's home, and the dirt around it, can be called a factory. This factory makes a special kind of dirt called topsoil.

Millipedes, spiders, and many other tiny insects live in a worm's home. It's like an insect highway. We might call the walls plain old dirt, but they are really tiny bits of stone piled one on another. The pieces of rock are held together by a kind of cement called humus.

It is made of dead and decaying bodies of plants and tiny animals.

Small plants such as fungi and algae supply food for the hungry travelers. Fungi are the kinds of plants that grow on moldy bread. Algae grow in damp places. When the roots of plants die, they leave paths for water. Air also comes down the same pathways.

As the water trickles down, it washes the sides of the tiny stones. It washes over the humus and gathers minerals. This is called soil solution. It is full of the nutrients that plants need.

The soil solution, humus, and tiny rocks combine to make topsoil. Without topsoil, there could be no plants. Without plants, there could be no animals and insects on land. Without topsoil, earth would be an almost lifeless globe revolving in space.

Working the Night Shift

Honeybees and fuzzy bumblebees buzz softly as they travel from flower to flower, gathering sweet nectar on a warm summer's day. Ahhh . . . doesn't it remind you of summer vacation!

Bees are always fun to watch, and their work is very important. Bees are the best and most commonly noticed "pollen movers" for flowers. They are one of many animals that provide important "pollination services" for our crops and wild plants. Because people and wildlife depend on these plants and fruits, they depend on bees.

Pollination is the movement of pollen within a flower and between flowers to produce fruits and seeds. Pollen can be moved by wind or water, or more reliably by insects and other animals we call pollinators. When pollen grains land on the stigma (the female part of a flower that connects to the ovary), they germinate and move down a pollen tube to the ovary. If pollination and

10

fertilization take place, the flower slowly transforms into a big, juicy apple.

If bees and other pollinators did not move the pollen "dust" around, our meals and snacks would consist only of wind-pollinated cereals and grains. In fact, we can thank pollinators for bringing us about a third of the food we eat.

Busy Bees

Bees are some of the most familiar and most helpful of all the animals that pollinate flowers. Although most do their work during daylight hours, some bees work at night. Because most bees are fuzzy and have featherlike branched hairs, pollen grains get lodged in their "fur" when they land on a flower to drink its nectar. Pollination is a lucky accident! Bees go about collecting food, and pollination is what happens when they travel from flower to flower.

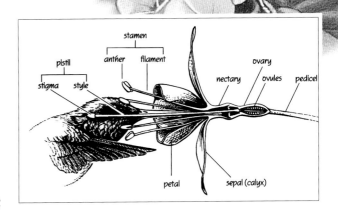

In the United States, there are about 4,000 different kinds of bees. Worldwide, scientists have named 25,000 kinds of bees. However, there are still many kinds of bees that have not

11

yet been discovered. Most bees live alone and nest in the ground or in twigs. Female ground-nesting bees collect their own pollen and nectar. Then they make it into a doughlike ball that they place on the bottom of a waterproof, underground cell. The mother bee then lays an egg on the pollen mixture, seals the cell with a mud cap, and goes on to build and fill other cells. Rarely does a mother bee have contact with her offspring. The baby bees emerge from their cells able to care for themselves.

Although many bees — especially those that live in deserts, or pollinate squash and pumpkin blossoms — get up very early in the morning, they don't really work at night. To find the bees with a real nightlife, let's travel to the rainforests of Costa Rica and Panama.

Fly-By-Night Pollinators

In these forests, some bees search for flowers after the sun goes down. They are found from Mexico to northern Argentina. They have pale-colored stomachs and fly at night, usually when there's bright moonlight. All bees have five eyes, but these night bees have greatly enlarged eyes, which help them see at night. Although they fly all night, they are busiest about two hours after sunset and then again an hour or so before dawn. To find their nests, you have to look closely among dead, broken sticks or vines, and especially in rotting wood.

Other night pollinators are seen more often. During a warm spring or summer night, sit quietly by a jasmine vine or some fragrant cactus flowers. You will see moths, attracted to the sweet-scented blossoms, coming for a drink. Bring a flashlight with red cellophane over the lens, and you can watch the moths without interfering with your night vision.

Most likely you will see the white-lined sphinx moth. Moths of this kind are often called hawk moths. Although the vast majority fly at night, some are like bumblebees and fly during daylight hours. You may be more familiar with these creatures in their newly hatched form. The big green tobacco and tomato hornworms that eat plants in your garden are the young forms of these fast-flying, beautiful moths.

When you spot a sphinx moth at a flower, watch how it flies with its tongue out, ready for action. It will come to a quick stop in front of a flower and then extend its tongue deep into the floral tubes to reach the thin, sweet nectar. Maybe you'll be lucky enough to see clumps of pollen on its tongue as it backs out of the flower. Often this type of moth will visit many flowers in a patch before flying elsewhere. Notice how it hovers in front of a blossom. If a small moth approaches a very large flower, it sometimes lands and crawls into the flower to reach the nectar.

Bees and Moths Can't Do It Alone

There are about 200,000 different kinds of animals that visit flowers in search of food. Among the invertebrate animals are bees, beetles, butterflies, flies, moths, and wasps. Vertebrate animals, such as birds and bats, can also be pollinators. There is even a gecko lizard that pollinates plants at night on islands off the coast of New Zealand. You probably have seen a tiny colorful hummingbird eagerly sipping nectar from a bright red tubular flower such as honeysuckle. If you live in a desert area such as Arizona, you are likely to have seen a long-nosed bat drinking nectar from giant cactus flowers at night. What a sight! You can thank bats in the warmer areas of the world for pollinating banana plants and many other kinds of fruit trees.

Save the Pollinators

Bees and other pollinators are in trouble around the world. As people turn wild lands into croplands, parking lots, roads, and housing tracts, there is less and less space for pollinators and their food plants. Today, we have fewer honeybee colonies than ever before. Some mites that came from Asia are now killing honeybees in the United States. They're threatening the livelihood of many beekeepers, as well as fruit and vegetable production. Pesticides also kill lots of pollinators and often poison our food and water supplies. Think about what you can do to help save the pollinators.

Circle of Life

A tiny caterpillar crawls out of an egg.

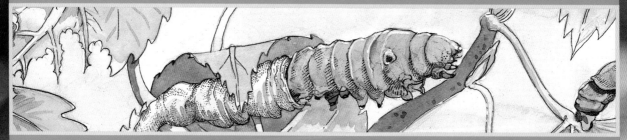

It eats and grows and sheds its skin four times.

Now it is a chrysalis, with a hard shell to protect it during the winter.

In spring an adult tiger swallowtail butterfly emerges to sip nectar and mate and lay eggs.

The queen bee lays an egg in a cell.

A larva hatches and is fed by worker bees. The larva spins a cocoon and grows.

The adult bee eats the wax covering its cell and begins to help care for the hive.

It gathers flower nectar to make honey and pollen to make food for new larvae.

When the hive is full, it follows the queen to a new hive, where the queen bee lays an egg . . .

An Eye for Ants

"Most people have a bug period. I never grew out of mine."

Dr. Edward O. Wilson, scientist and teacher, has spent his life peeking into the nests of ants. He's curious about the job of each ant in the colony. He wants to uncover the secrets of ant colonies' success.

As a child, Edward was often alone. His mother and father separated. He had to move many times. In 11 years, he went to 14 different schools! Wherever he lived, snakes, fish, and insects became his friends. For a time, he even kept a colony of harvester ants in a jar under his bed.

The summer he was seven, Edward hurt his

This is good!

Did you know?
Most ants are scavengers. They find food outside the nest.

Hey, save some for the rest of us!

Great find!

right eye in a fishing accident. As he says, "The attention of my surviving eye turned to the ground." It wasn't long before Edward decided to become a scientist who studies insects.

Ants live almost everywhere — from tropical climates to beyond the Arctic Circle, from dry deserts to shady rainforests, from city sidewalks to wild woodlands, and from deep in the ground to the tops of the tallest trees. They live in colonies. An ant colony can have as many as 20 million members.

There is only one queen ant in a colony. It's the queen's task to lay the eggs. Out of the eggs grow worker ants and sometimes a new queen. Every ant in a colony has a job. The main goal of all the worker ants is to take care of the queen and her offspring. This they do in some amazing ways.

For 40 years, Edward has traveled around the world looking for new kinds of ants. Sometimes he brings entire colonies back to his laboratory

Did You Know?
Some kinds of ants actually "farm" their food. Some "farming" ants grow fungus on underground leaf farms.

in order to observe them more closely. He wants to learn about each ant's job within its colony. He wants to know how each ant's job helps the species to survive in the future.

Edward's discoveries help us understand why many animal species develop ways of living in groups. Each member of the group has certain jobs. Each job is important to the entire species' success.

Whenever possible, Edward still returns to the place where he first watched ants. He notices the changes in ant species that have occurred over the past 60 years. And today he still relies on what he saw and collected when he was a young boy.

An Ant Experiment to Try

Worker ants must build, feed, and guard their colony. To do this they need to communicate with each other. Like most living things, ants depend on chemical odors to send messages such as, "I found food over here" or "This ant looks dead — take him out," or "Alert! There's a stranger in here." Over the

Did you know?
Some queen ants live a long time. But the worker ants that bring the queen's food usually live for only a week or so.

years, Edward has carried out hundreds of experiments to find the meanings of these odor signals. He has made many important discoveries, but many mysteries remain to be solved.

You can do an experiment to test the odor signals of ants. Put several drops of sugar water on a piece of paper. Place the paper near some ants. Watch as one ant discovers the food. Other ants will soon follow the first ant's odor trail. Turn the paper sideways. The ants will still follow the scent of the odor trail, although the sugar water is now in a different place.

Did you know?
There are ants that "milk" drops of sugar, called "honeydew," from aphids.

Laurel's Rainforest

L aurel smiled. This was her first morning in the Costa Rican rainforest. All day yesterday she and her mom had been on airplanes and buses and bumpy vans. Now they were finally at the rainforest research station, where her father was a visiting scientist.

Mom came out onto the porch. "Ready?" she asked. Her parents thought Laurel should take it easy today, after all her traveling. But Laurel couldn't wait to explore the rainforest. She wanted Daddy to take her all the way up to the platforms, built high above the rainforest floor, where he did most of his research!

At first, all Laurel could see was green. Tall, tall trees made a green roof above her head. Twisty vines and giant ferns and soft, lush blankets of moss grew everywhere. The air was moist and steamy against her face.

"It can get pretty muddy here," Daddy warned. "It's not called a rainforest for nothing — once it rained 14 times in the same day! If you slip, don't grab

for a tree — it might be covered with biting ants or sharp spines. Just go ahead and fall in the mud."

That sounded like fun.

Laurel looked more closely at a twisty trunk on the edge of the path. Sure enough, it was covered with what looked like pointy

23

green and brown leaves. "Daddy!" she called. "Like these spines?"

Her father came to look. "Good eyes, Laurel!" he said. "But these aren't spines — they're bugs! They're called treehoppers. They look like sharp spines, so birds and animals won't want to eat them."

Bugs that looked like spines! Laurel watched, fascinated. The treehoppers covered that trunk, and they didn't move a bit. Laurel stood quietly for a long time. Around her, rainforest noises filled the air. Whistles and chirps and buzzing, squawks and shufflings and tap-tap-taps.

Laurel looked up. Rainforest trees didn't look very much like the maple and apple trees she climbed at home.

"I'd have to be a monkey to climb these —" she started to say, and then snapped her mouth shut in astonishment. There were monkeys right here! Right above her head!

Laurel watched those monkeys for a long time, and then she and her parents started moving back up the path. But Laurel stopped again almost immediately. She squatted and peered at the ground.

"Daddy!" she called again. "Come see!"

It was the funniest thing. A parade of ants was marching by the side of the path. Each ant looked like it was wearing a green leaf hat on its head. The ants didn't turn left and they didn't turn right. They just trooped

25

forward with their green hats, looking for
all the world like the cartoon ants in one
of Laurel's favorite movies.

Mom and Daddy squatted to look, too.
"Leafcutter ants," Daddy announced.
"They climb clear up to the tops of the trees
to bite off pieces of leaves, then they carry
them all the way down to their underground
home. Then the ants make a kind of
moldy garden with their leaves,
and that's what they eat."

It sounded yucky.

But still — "That's a long
walk," Laurel said.

"Yep," Daddy agreed.
"Kind of like if you
climbed all the way

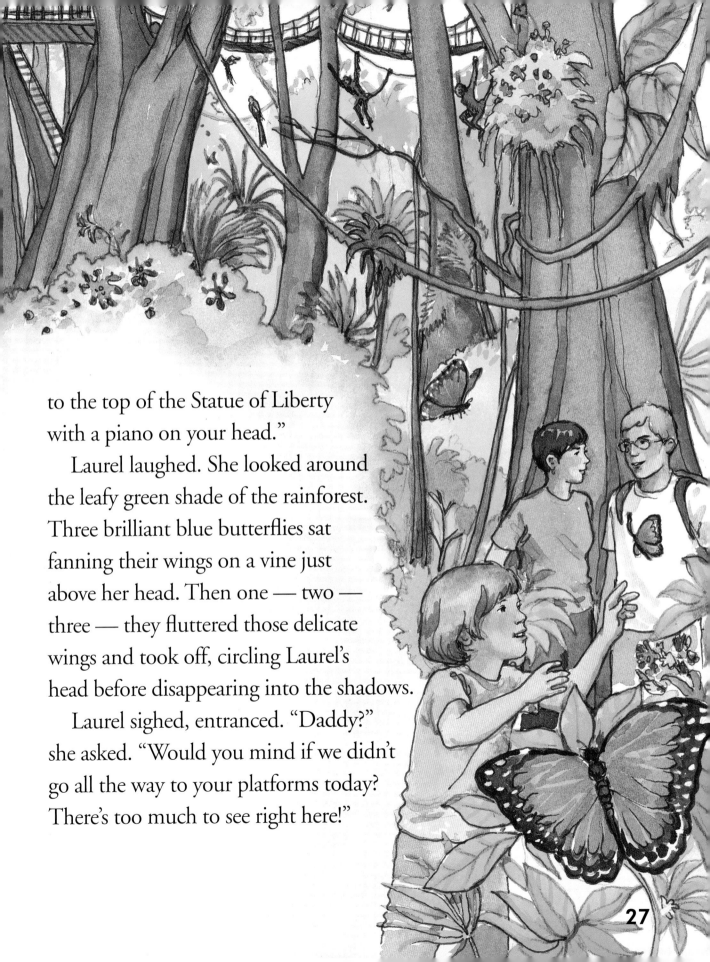

to the top of the Statue of Liberty with a piano on your head."

Laurel laughed. She looked around the leafy green shade of the rainforest. Three brilliant blue butterflies sat fanning their wings on a vine just above her head. Then one — two — three — they fluttered those delicate wings and took off, circling Laurel's head before disappearing into the shadows.

Laurel sighed, entranced. "Daddy?" she asked. "Would you mind if we didn't go all the way to your platforms today? There's too much to see right here!"

27

Tricky Animals

What big eyes you have! That's what a hungry bird thinks when a silk moth opens its wings. The moth's false eyespots look like the eyes of an owl and can frighten an attacker away.

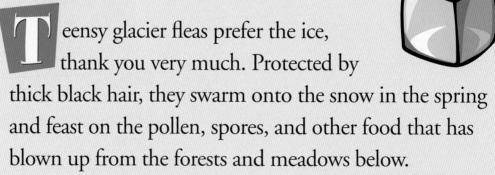

Glad to "flea" ya!

Teensy glacier fleas prefer the ice, thank you very much. Protected by thick black hair, they swarm onto the snow in the spring and feast on the pollen, spores, and other food that has blown up from the forests and meadows below.

Glossary

Colony

Aphid: a small, soft-bodied insect that sucks sap from plants.

Camouflage: coloring that looks like something else.

Chrysalis: a protected stage of growth when a caterpillar changes into a butterfly.

Colony: a group of the same kind of animal.

Communicate: to talk or exchange ideas.

Experiment: a test used to show a known truth.

Harvester: one who gathers a crop.

Invertebrate: animals that do not have a backbone or spine.

Laboratory: a room or building used for science experiments.

Larva: a newly hatched, wingless, wormlike form of an insect.

Millipede: an insect with many legs.

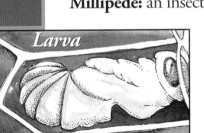
Larva

Minerals: materials that are not plant or animal.

Nectar: a sweet liquid produced by flowers.

Nutritious: providing nourishment — food.

Pesticide: any substance used to kill insects and other small forms of life.

Harvester

Pollen: fine, powderlike material made by part of the flower of a seed plant.

Research: to do close, careful study.

Scavenger: an animal that feeds on dead or decaying plants or animals.

Solution: a mixture of materials.

Vertebrate: animals that have a backbone or spine.

Nectar

The World of BUGS

North America

United States

Arizona

Mexico

Costa Rica

Panama

Atlantic Ocean

Amazon

South

America

Argentina

Pacific

Ocean

N
W   E
S

Europe

Asia

Africa

Indian

Ocean

Australia

New Zealand

Antarctica

Animals are Amazing!

All around the world, animals roam on the earth, in the sky, and under the water. Come explore the fascinating world of animals through a unique collection of stories inspired from the pages of *CLICK*® magazine. Travel with us as we meet many types of animals and discover all the amazing ways they enhance our world.

$17⁹⁵ each

Titles in the Animal Series

BUGS

PETS

WATER ANIMALS

WILD ANIMALS

Sea Star

Sea Star grips the rocky ocean bottom near shore. Waves crash over her, but she holds on tight. Tiny suckers underneath her five arms keep her in place. The suckers are on the tips of hundreds of little tubes that Sea Star uses as feet to crawl along the ocean floor.

The ocean waves carry the smell of clams to her. Sea Star is always ready for a meal. Her muscles pull water inside her body. Her tube feet fill like little balloons, and their suckers grab onto the sea floor. Then Sea Star squeezes the water out of some of her tube feet to pull herself forward. By pumping water in and out, Sea Star creeps closer and closer to the smell of clams.

When Sea Star reaches her goal, she climbs on top of a clam. The clam snaps its two shells closed, hiding its soft body. Clamping on with her tube feet, Sea Star tries to pry the shells open. She pulls and pulls, but the clam's strong muscles hold tight. Finally, Sea Star budges the shells apart.

Sea Star flips her stomach out through the mouth on her underside and into the tiny gap between the clam's body. She squirts chemicals that soften the clam's body. When the clam turns soupy, she swallows her meal. All that remains are two empty shells.

After finishing her meal, Sea Star clings